3 Wise Men and a Baby

A Children's Christmas Musical teaching that the best gift is me!

created by

Pam Andrews

LILLENAS
PUBLISHING COMPANY

lillenas.com

CONTENTS

Cast

Wise Man 1 (Elvistonia)

Wise Man 2 (Garthonia)

Wise Man 3 (Jamestonia)

Star

Twink

Sparklett

Glow

Scribe

Lydia

Martha

Townsperson 1

Townsperson 2

Herod

Joseph

Townspeople

Kid 1

Kid 2

Kid 3

Kid 4

Non-Speaking Cast

Mary

2-3 Shepherds

Setting

Center Stage

Opening, Jerusalem, and Bethlehem

Stage Right

King Herod scene

Mary and Joseph's house

Stage Left

Star scene

Overture

It's Christmas
Lookin' for a King

Arranged by John M. DeVries

8

*"Lookin' for a King"

*Music by PAM ANDREWS. Copyright © 2004 by Pilot Point Music (ASCAP). All rights reserved. Administered by The Copyright Company, 1025 16th Avenue South, Nashville, TN 37212.

10

(handwritten) Split trax. With voices

Jesus Is Born

(handwritten) start music @ "This tiny baby"

Words and Music by
PAM ANDERWS
Arranged by John M. DeVries

Ethereal ♩= ca. 86

CD: 2

(handwritten) Courtney

*STAR: Long ago in a quiet little town called Bethlehem, the world was changed forever. Jesus Christ, our Savior, was born. A simple star led the way. This tiny Baby, born to Mary, His Mother, was worshipped by shepherds and circled by angels. But, that was not the end of the story. Others would come to worship the new King. Wise Men traveled from a far away land to meet Jesus and give Him gifts. The journey of these Wise Men to Jesus is a wonderful story the whole world should know.

3rd time to Coda
(to pg. 16, meas. 66)

CD: 6 / 8 / 10   1st / 2nd / 3rd time

Je - sus is born! Ho - san - na to the King!

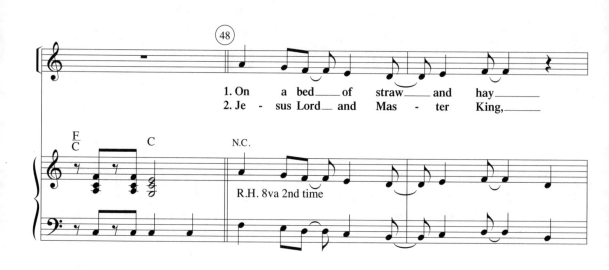

1. On a bed of straw and hay
2. Je - sus Lord and Mas - ter King,

R.H. 8va 2nd time

Je - sus came the world to save. Came to earth to make
Fa - ther God of ev - 'ry - thing Makes me want to shout

_ a way___ For us to live___ with Him.___
_ and sing___ Ho - san - na, He___ is born.___

Gm6/E   A7♭9

Nev - er cry - ing, not___ a sound,___ An - gels hov - er all___
Teach - er, Lord___ and Ho - ly One,___ Sav - ior, and___ God's on -

N.C.

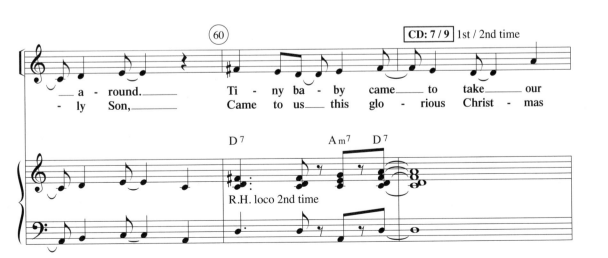

_ a - round.___ Ti - ny ba - by came___ to take___ our
- ly Son,___ Came to us___ this glo - rious Christ - mas

CD: 7 / 9   1st / 2nd time

D7   Am7   D7

R.H. loco 2nd time

16

Scene 1

Courtney

STAR: Today our Savior is born! Is everyone ready to celebrate?

Bailey

TWINK: Not quite, Star. Sparklett is still working on the cake.

STAR: Don't dillydally, Sparklett. We want our Lord's birthday cake to be the best ever.

Harley

SPARKLETT *(with a French accent)*: Just za few more star sparkles zand we'll be ready. *(sprinkles sparkles on the birthday cake.)*

STAR: Twink, how are you and your fellow stars coming with the gift.

TWINK: That's a tough one, Star. What do you give someone who made it all? (Glow *brings out wrapping paper, ribbon, and a box. He also has a clipboard and pencil.)*

STAR: Jesus is always grateful for any gift. Even the smallest of gifts makes Him happy.

TWINK: He's <u>so</u> wonderful. I just want His birthday present to be perfect.

STAR: Jesus will love whatever you give Him, Twink. What are some of your ideas?

TWINK: Glow, will you read us your list?

Diana

GLOW: Yes, boss. *(reads from a clipboard)* We thought about a crown, *(pulls a crown from the box)* but any crown we came up with looked pale to the ones He already has. We thought about a sweater, *(pulls a sweater from the box)* but in heaven it's never cold.

STAR: What about a heavenly tie?

GLOW: Don't you remember? We gave Him a tie last year. *(pulls a tie from the box)*

TWINK: And the year before that…

GLOW: And the year before that…

TWINK: What about giving Him a gold watch? *(pulls a watch from the box)*

GLOW: The Wise Men already gave Him gold, frankincense, and myrrh, so that's out.

STAR: Glow, the Wise Men gave Jesus more than gold, frankincense, and myrrh.

TWINK: What are you talking about, Star? It says clearly here in Matthew 2 that they brought gold, frankincense, and myrrh.

STAR: Yes, they did bring those wonderful gifts, Twink, but they gave so much more.

SPARKLETT: Ah! Ze Wise Men were– how do you say– superb! Za story of za Wise Men is zwonderful!

STAR: It certainly is, Sparklett. This story might just be the thing to get us thinking in the right direction for the perfect gift for our Lord. Come stars, gather around and I will tell you the story.

TWINK: We would appreciate your help, Star.

GLOW: And would love to hear the story.

STAR: OK. Well, as many of you know, I was the star on duty that night 2000 years ago. Little did I know that I would be the star that led the people to Jesus. I was ordered to shine on Bethlehem the moment Jesus was born.

GLOW: How wonderful!

STAR: Yes, it was wonderful. I remember gathering every bit of star power from the Lord I could hold. That is the brightest that I have ever shined. Jesus was born! Our Savior was born!

(During GO, TELL IT ON THE MOUNTAIN, MARY, *holding Baby Jesus, and* JOSEPH *appear stage right in a simple manger scene.* SHEPHERDS *join the scene and* ANGELS *are dancing. This should be a celebration.)*

Go, Tell It on the Mountain

JOHN W. WORK, JR.

Afro-American Spiritual
Arranged by John M. DeVries

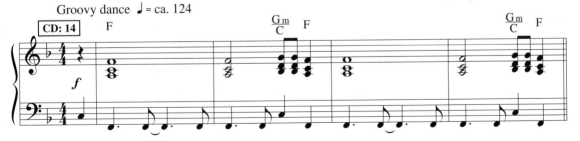

Groovy dance ♩ = ca. 124

CD: 14

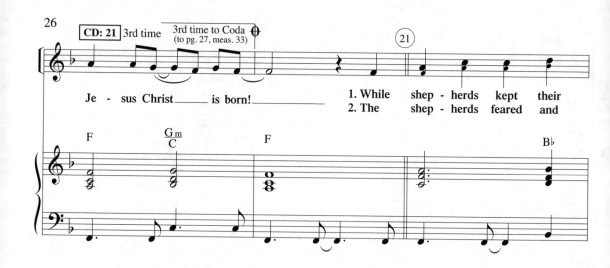

3rd time to Coda (to pg. 27, meas. 33)

CD: 21 3rd time

Je - sus Christ___ is born!___

1. While shep - herds kept their
2. The shep - herds feared and

watch - ing O'er si - lent flocks by___ night, Be -
trem - bled When lo! a - bove the___ earth Rang

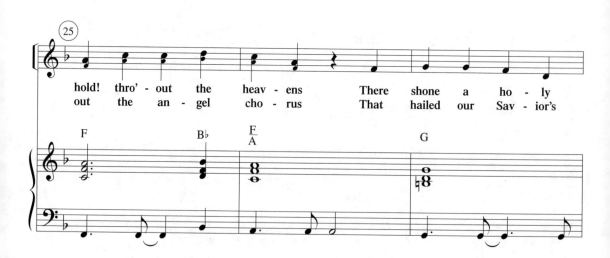

hold! thro' - out the heav - ens There shone a ho - ly
out the an - gel cho - rus That hailed our Sav - ior's

28

Scene 2

Dalton

STAR: Yes, Jesus was born that wonderful night. Shepherds came to worship Jesus.

GLOW: Led, of course, by Star. *(points to the star)*

Taylor B.

SPARKLETT: But, ze story does not end zat ze manger, does zit, Star?

Jonathan Green

STAR: You are right, Sparklett. There was more. I can remember it as if it were yesterday. In the
Peyton days after Jesus was born, Joseph moved his family into a little house on the edge of
town. They now had a home in Bethlehem. But Joseph feared that his family was not
safe. The news of Jesus' birth had spread all across the land. Joseph and Mary knew
that after the shepherds came, there would be more visitors wanting to meet Jesus.
Some of the visitors would just be curious. Some would come and worship Jesus just
as the shepherds. But, they also knew some would want to harm Jesus.

Taylor

TWINK: But not the Wise Men. They wanted to worship Jesus, right Star?

STAR: Yes, Twink. There were three Wise Men, kings if you will. It is thought that they came
Courtney from some far off place in the Orient. Because they were astronomers, they had noticed
me shining in the heavens.

TWINK: I would've loved to see you shine like that.

STAR: They left their homes and riches to investigate this new star. They met each other on the
way and found they were all following the same star. They heard on the way that this
Connor star had appeared when a new king had been born.

(music begins. WISE MAN 1 *enters from down one aisle and the other* WISE MEN *enter from
another aisle. They meet each other on stage right. The* WISE MEN *should ride camel stick
horses or camels made from boxes.)*

Traveling Afar Part 1

Unknown
Arranged by John M. DeVries

pause music

WISE MAN 1: Like, hello, fellow wise dudes. *(bows to* WISE MAN 2 *and* 3*)*

WISE MAN 2: Howdy. *(bows to* WISE MAN 1, *who tips his hat)*

WISE MAN 3: Hello, wise brothers. *(bows to* WISE MAN 1*)*

WISE MAN 1 *(in an Elvis style voice)*: Thank you, thank you very much. I'm Elvistonia. Philosophy is the thing I do. I've been travellin' from the far east followin' that star. I'm from the Land of the Angels, also called L.A. Aren't you two also from the Orient like me?

WISE MAN 2: Sure thing, partner, we too are travelers. We met a few miles back. We've both been followin' that there star. I am from the southern Orient. My name is Garthonia. My homeland is Bucksnort, Persia.

WISE MAN 3: Hey, fellow wise brothers. I'm Jamestonia. I'm a healer of body and soul. I come from the land of Motown, Chaldea. I "heard it through the grapevine" that the one who will be King of the Jews has been born. *(points to the star)* I believe that star will lead us to the Christ Child. I want to find Him and worship Him.

WISE MAN 1: Come on. Let's hit the road together and find this new King. *(The* WISE MEN *begin to walk.)* Elvistonia has left the Orient.

We Three Kings

Words and Music by
JOHN H. HOPKINS, JR.
and PAM ANDREWS
Arranged by John M. DeVries

CD: 27

wise men three, they're search-ing for their King.

Dm6 A7b9 Dm6 A7b9 Dm6

11 *Wise Men* *mf*

We three kings___of Or-i-ent are;_____ Bear-ing gifts___we tra-verse a-far___

N.C.

(Drums)

CD: 28

Field and foun - tain, moor and moun - tain– Fol-low-ing yon - der star.

Wise Men and Choir

O_____ star of won - der, star of night,

C7 F Fsus F

Star with roy - al beau-ty bright, West-ward lead - ing, still pro-ceed - ing,

F   F sus   F   D m   C   B♭   C

CD: 29

Guide us to thy per-fect light.

F   F sus   F   N.C.

(Drums)

22 *Wise Man 1* *mf*

I'm a wise man from the east; Through

rocks and hills I seek the King. Phil - os - o-phy is what I know– I'm

CD: 30

Fast rock ♩ = ca. 170

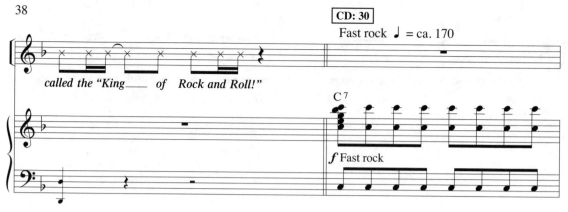

called the "King___ of Rock and Roll!"

Wise Man 1 and Choir

Star of won - der,

star of night, Star with

roy - al beau - ty bright,

All this trav - el makes me hun - gry, That's why I'm called__ the "King of Coun - try."

Bluegrass feel in 2 ♩ = ca. 124

49 C7

CD: 32

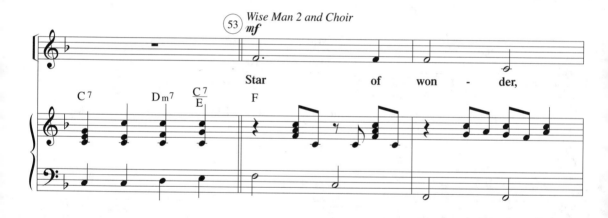

53 *Wise Man 2 and Choir*
mf

C7 Dm7 C7/E F

Star   of   won   -   der,

57

star   of   night,   Star   with

B♭   F

70 *Wise Man 3*
mf

I'm a wise___man from the East,___ I help the sick___and those in need. My

heart de-sires___ my King to know, That's why I'm called___the "King of Soul."

74 Funky soul beat ♩ = ca. 180
N.C.
CD: 34
f

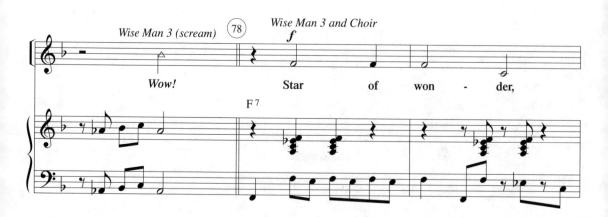

Wise Man 3 (scream) **78** *Wise Man 3 and Choir*
f

Wow! Star of won - der,

F⁷

per - fect light.

Bb   N.C.

93 Like beginning ♩ = ca. 100

mf Like beginning

CD: 35

97 *Choir*
mf

Wise men three, they trav - el from the East, They

Dm6   A7♭9   Dm6   A7♭9   Dm6

100

nev - er rest, they nev - er stop, They ride their cam - els till they drop, They're

BbM7   Gm9   Gm6/E   A7♭9

Star with roy - al beau-ty bright, West-ward lead - ing, still pro-ceed - ing,

Guide us to_____thy per-fect light. West-ward lead - ing, still pro-ceed - ing,

Guide us to___ thy per-fect light. *Yea!*

Scene 3

TWINK: What a great story, Star! Wasn't it amazing that these Wise Men all knew that if they followed the star they would find Jesus?

SPARKLETT: Oui, zat was zo amazing.

GLOW: Simply amazing.

STAR: God was really leading the Wise Men. He just used me as a tool to help them along. And, the Wise Men had real courage. Just imagine leaving your homeland to follow a star. The Wise Men traveled over hills and valleys. They traveled through sand storms and cold nights. But, they did not give up. They knew that finding Jesus and having Him in their lives was the most important thing that would ever happen to them.

SPARKLETT: Ze Wise Men were zo very wise!!

TWINK: Very wise!!

GLOW: Very, very wise!!!

STAR: The Wise Men followed me, the star, to Jerusalem. When they got to the city, they began asking the townspeople about Jesus.

(music begins. TOWNSPEOPLE appear center stage. The WISE MEN move briefly down the aisle and then to center stage. TOWNSPEOPLE roll in the Jerusalem set. The Herod set [a chair] is stage right. HEROD sits in the chair.)

Traveling Afar Part 2

Unknown
Arranged by John M. DeVries

Persian feel ♩ = ca. 100

WISE MAN 1: Ah, Jerusalem...

WISE MAN 1: Ah, Jerusalem. What a rockin' city.

WISE MAN 2: I am sooooo tired. *(rubs backside)* I'm sure I'm gettin' a saddle sore. I'm glad we're finally in a city. I could use some grub.

WISE MAN 3: Soul food, brother! Soul food!

WISE MAN 1: Focus, O wise ones. We are seeking the newborn King. Do you think we should ask for directions?

WISE MAN 2: Who ever heard of a Wise "Man" asking fer directions?

WISE MAN 1: But maybe these townspeople have some information about the new King that will help us find our way.

WISE MAN 3: Mercy me! It wouldn't hurt to try. Hey, excuse me, brother.

SCRIBE *(very proper)*: Yes…

WISE MAN 1: Hey, Scribe, dude. Have you heard of a new King being born? We've been following that star and it has led us here to Jerusalem.

SCRIBE: The only king around here is King Herod. And he definitely is not a newborn. I'm sorry, I must not tarry. I have important business to attend to.*(exits stage right to* KING HEROD. *He pretends to talk to* HEROD.*)*

WISE MAN 2: Come on, folks, some of you must've heard of the new King. They say He'll be the King of the Jews.

WISE MAN 3: We Wise Brothers want to give Him gifts and worship Him. Are you sure you haven't seen Him?

TOWNSPERSON 1: No, I haven't seen any king.

TOWNSPERSON 2: I haven't either.

WISE MAN 1: Can't any of you help us? We're lookin' for a King!

Lookin' for a King

with
Joy to the World

Words and Music by
PAM ANDREWS
Arranged by John M. DeVries

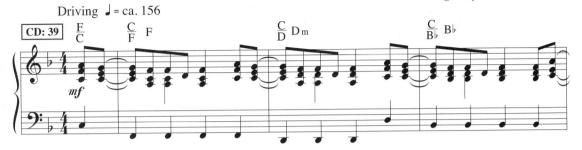

51

54

CD: 45

C   Gm9/C   C/F   F

Dm7   Dm   C/B♭   B♭

C   F   CM7/D   D/G   G

D/E   Em   D/C   C

-sus.   We're look - in' for a king   and prais-

-es we will bring, we're look - in' for a king   named Je-

-sus.   We're look - in' for a king,   we're look-

-in' for a king,   we're look - in' for a king   named Je-

Scene 4

STAR: Now, when King Herod heard about this new King, He was troubled.

TWINK: That King Herod was not very nice. There was no twinkle in his eyes.

SPARKLETT: No sparkle zin zis crown.

GLOW: No glow in his eyes.

STAR: He sent for the wise men to appear before him. He wanted to learn more about this new King. (SCRIBE *moves to center stage*)

Scribe: Excuse me, wise travelers from the East. I want to invite you to King Herod's palace. I have spoken to him and he is anxious to hear about this new King. Come with me.

WISE MAN 1: I guess we could take a few minutes out of our journey to meet your King Herod, dude.

WISE MAN 2: Shucks, yeah.

WISE MAN 3: Maybe he can whip us up some soul food.

(Music begins. WISE MEN *move to stage right to meet* HEROD.*)*

meet Herod

Traveling Afar Part 3

Unknown
Arranged by John M. DeVries

WISE MAN 1: Hey, Herod, main dude. What a rockin' pad you have here.

WISE MAN 2: Nice to meet ya, partner. *(shakes hands with HEROD)*

WISE MAN 3: Like the threads, Bro.

HEROD: Welcome. What brings you Wise Men to my city?

WISE MAN 1: We've traveled from the east following that bright star. *(points to the star)*

WISE MAN 2: We're searchin' for the new King…the King of the Jews.

WISE MAN 3: We saw His star in the east and have come to worship Him.

HEROD: This is the first I've heard of this new King. *(slyly)* I, too, would like to worship Him. Once you find him, you must return to Jerusalem and tell me about Him. Then, I can meet him, too.

WISE MAN 1: No prob, Herod. We can swing back by, but, I'm afraid we must be on our way.

WISE MAN 3: Catch you later, King Brother.

WISE MAN 2: Yep, it's time to hit the trail. Let's head 'em up and move 'em out.

(During STAR, LEAD US TO JESUS, *the* WISE MEN *travel until they reach the Bethlehem scene. The Herod scene is rotated to Joseph's house.)*

wisemen travel — sign to change Joseph's house

Star, Lead Us to Jesus

with

We Three Kings

Words and Music by
PAM ANDREWS
Arranged by John M. DeVries

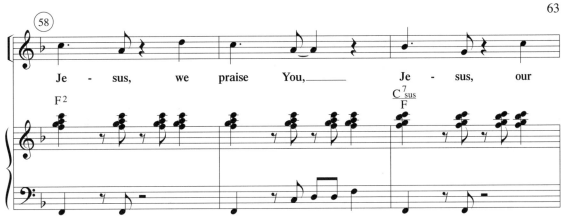

Je - sus, we praise You,_____ Je - sus, our

King; Je - sus, we love You, our

CD: 53

gifts we_____ do bring. Star, lead_____ us to

Choir 2

Je - sus, our

Je - sus, _____ star, show __ us the way;

Sav - ior, _____ Je - sus, our Lord;

Star, lead __ us to Je - sus, star, lead __ us to -

Je - sus, Re - deem - er, the Child we a -

day. Let's get __ our - selves mov - ing,

dore. Je - sus, we praise You, _____

no time to de - lay; Star, lead us to

Je - sus, our King; Je - sus, we

Je - sus, star, lead us to - day.

love You, our gifts we do bring.

Star of won - der, Guide us to thy

Star of won - der,

Scene 5

(The Jerusalem sign is turned to Bethlehem. The well is moved into place. The WISE MEN move to center stage.)

WISE MAN 1: Bethlehem. Who would have thought that the star would lead us here.

WISE MAN 2: I'm so tired. I know we've stopped to catch a few winks on the trail, but I didn't sleep very well. I kept havin' this here strange dream. There was this voice telling me not to go back to that King Herod.

WISE MAN 3: Bless my soul, I had the same dream.

WISE MAN 1: Me, too. I guess that means we'll take that northern detour around Jerusalem when we return home and can that return appearance in front of that King Herod Dude.

(Enter MARTHA *and* LYDIA *center stage. They carry baskets.*

LYDIA: Martha, hurry. We must gather water from the well for Mother.

MARTHA: Ok, Lydia. We can have this done in no time.

LYDIA *(whispering)*: Look, Martha. Strangers.

MARTHA *(whispering)*: They are royalty. Kings!

LYDIA: Magi!

MARTHA: Wise Men!

WISE MAN 1: Hey, little ladies!

LYDIA: Yes, your majesty. *(curtsies)*

MARTHA: Yes, your highness. *(curtsies)*

WISE MAN 1: Thank you! Thank you very much, little ladies. We are Wise Men. We have
   traveled from the east following that bright star.

WISE MAN 2: We're searchin' fer a King…the King of the Jews.

WISE MAN 3: Yes, little sister. We saw His star in the east and have come to get down and
   worship Him.

LYDIA: You must mean Jesus. He was born some months ago in the innkeeper's stable.

WISE MAN 1: Are you girls sure He is the King? What King would be born in a stable?

LYDIA: Oh, He doesn't live in a stable anymore. He lives with Mary and Joseph in a little house
   on the edge of town.

MARTHA: But, you are right about Jesus. There's something very special about this Baby.
   People are saying that He will be the new King of the Jews.

LYDIA: All I know is that He is an awesome little Boy.

MARTHA: Sometimes when His mother Mary goes to the market, we get to sit with Him. He's
   soooooo cute.

LYDIA: I just love to rock Him.

MARTHA: His eyes are filled with love.

Rockin' Baby Jesus

Words and Music by
PAM ANDREWS
Arranged by John M. DeVries

Praise the Lord, wor - ship and a - dore;

Al - le - lu - ia, al - le - lu - ia, al - le - lu - ia.

Al - le - lu, al - le - lu - ia.

46 All · · · · · · · · · CD: 62

Je - sus Christ is born. Je - sus Christ is born.

50

Wor - ship Je - sus, wor - ship Ba - by Je - sus. Wor - ship

B#9#5 Em A Em A

Scene 6

LYDIA: Come with us. We will take you to Him.

MARTHA: You will love Him. And believe it or not, You will know He loves you, too. He's amazing. *(LYDIA and MARTHA exit)*

WISE MAN 1: Is my crown straight? I want to look my best. Give me a minute to shine this gold.

WISE MAN 2: Let me slick down my hair and dust off this box of frankincense.

WISE MAN 3 *(panicked)*: Bros, where's my myrrh? *(finds it in his bag)* Ah, thank, goodness. I thought I might've lost it in the last sandstorm.

WISE MAN 1: When we meet Him, what should we do?

WISE MAN 2: I might just bow.

WISE MAN 3: I might sing to Him.

WISE MAN 1: Just imagine, my friends. We are about to meet our King. *(WISE MEN exit stage right.)*

use tape

I Can Only Imagine

Words and Music by
BART MILLARD
Arranged by John M. DeVries

82

Scene 7

(MARY and JOSEPH appear stage right. MARY is holding a baby wrapped in cloth. The WISE MEN enter with MARTHA and LYDIA.)

WISE MAN 1: Hello, sir.

JOSEPH: Why have you come?

WISE MAN 1: We have followed that star to the new King, Jesus. We've come to bring Him gifts and worship Him.

JOSEPH: You are welcome here. Mary and I know that we have been entrusted with a blessed Child. Thank you for travelling so far to visit us.

WISE MAN 1: I bring the Child gold. *(hands JOSEPH the gold)*

WISE MAN 2: I bring Him frankincense… *(hands JOSEPH the frankincense)*

WISE MAN 3: And I bring myrrh. *(hands JOSEPH the myrrh)*

WISE MAN 1: But there is one more thing I want to give to the Christ Child. *(to the child)* I give You my heart, Jesus.

WISE MAN 2: And I give you my love.

WISE MAN 3: And I give you my worship. *(The WISE MEN kneel and worship Jesus.)*

STAR: You see, stars? The Wise Men gave Jesus their hearts. They gave Jesus their love. They gave their worship.

TWINK: I see, Star. They gave Jesus their all. We stars will make every beam of light that comes from us be a Jesus light. That will be our gift to Jesus this Christmas.

Sparklett: Zimply marvelous!!!

Glow: What a shining idea!

Star: Truly the best gift anyone can give to Jesus is themselves.

Twink: Who would have ever thought that the best gift for Jesus would be me?

(During THE BEST GIFT IS ME, the WISE MEN kneel in front of Baby Jesus. At the end of the song, MARY, JOSEPH, WISE MEN and the STARS exit to the choir.)

The Best Gift Is Me

Words and Music by
PAM ANDREWS
Arranged by John M. DeVries

2nd time to Coda
(to pg. 90, meas. 48)

mer-ry Christ-mas, Je - sus,

I give You my heart.

Where can I buy___ a gift

that's wor-thy of___ Your love___ for me?___

I give You my heart.

Scene 8

STAR *(moves to center stage)*: What will you give Jesus this Christmas? Will you be like the Wise Men? Will you give Him your worship?

KID 1: In Matthew 2:11, the Bible says, "On coming to the house, they saw the child with his mother Mary, and they bowed down and worshiped him. Then they opened their treasures and presented him with gifts of gold and of incense and of myrrh."

STAR: The Wise Men worshipped Jesus and gave Him presents. We should also give of our earthly treasures like the Wise Men, but you have something Jesus wants more than anything precious found on this earth. He wants your heart.

KID 2: In Romans 10:9-10, the Bible says, "That if you confess with your mouth, 'Jesus is Lord,' and believe in your heart that God raised him from the dead, you will be saved. For it is with your heart that you believe and are justified, and it is with your mouth that you confess and are saved."

STAR: He wants your love.

KID 3: In Mark 12:30, the Bible says, "Love the Lord your God with all your heart and with all your soul and with all your mind and with all your strength."

STAR: He wants you.

KID 4: In 1 Corinthians 15:58, the Bible says, "Therefore, my dear brothers, stand firm. Let nothing move you. Always give yourselves fully to the work of the Lord, because you know that your labor in the Lord is not in vain."

STAR: Become a wise person. Worship Jesus this Christmas. Invite Him into your heart and life. Give Him your all and make this the best Christmas ever!

(Option: At this moment, you may have SPARKLETT bring out a birthday cake with a lit candle and have the audience sing "Happy Birthday" to Jesus.)

Finale

It's Christmas
Angels We Have Heard on High
I Can Only Imagine
Jesus Is Born

Arranged by John M. DeVries

*Words and Music by PAM ANDREWS. Copyright © 2004 by Pilot Point Music (ASCAP). All rights reserved. Administered by The Copyright Company, 1025 16th Avenue South, Nashville, TN 37212.

100

*"Jesus Is Born"

CD: 81

Praise the Lord,__ Ho-san-na! Praise the Lord,__ Ho-san-na, Je-sus Sav - ior is

born! Je-sus is born!__ Ho - san - na!

Solo

Ho - san - na!__

(Drum break)

Je-sus is born!__ Ho - san - na to the King! Je-sus is born!__ Ho-san-

Ho - san - na!__

Curtain Call

It's Christmas
Angels We Have Heard on High
I Can Only Imagine
Jesus Is Born

Arranged by John M. DeVries

*"Angels We Have Heard on High"

D.S. al Coda
(to pg. 109, meas. 5)

**"I Can Only Imagine"
Slower ♩ = ca. 84

CODA

CD: 85

mf

I can on-ly im-a-gine.

Surrounded by___ Your glo-ry, what

will my___ heart feel?___ Will I dance___ for You Je-sus, or in

awe of You___ be still?___ Will I stand___ in___ Your pre-sence, or to my

99

Je-sus is born! Ho - san - na!

Je-sus is born! Ho - san -

Ho - san - na!

103

- na to the King! Je-sus is born! Ho - san - na!

Ho - san - na!

Ho - san - na!

103

CD: 89

Je-sus is born! Ho - san - na to the King!

Ho - san - na to the King!

C

D/C G/D

Joy to the world, ho - san - na to the

King!

PRODUCTION NOTES

For more production details please refer to "3 Wise Men and a Baby Director's Resource Kit" or the "3 Wise Men and a Baby Video."

Setting

The set for "Three Wise Men and a Baby" is designed in three basic and simple areas on stage. Stage left will be the Star Scene. To create this scene, drape white sheets over crates and accent with white quilt batting. Paint an insulation board white or cover it with a white plastic table cloth. This will stand behind the angel scene. It would be nice to add shiny stars to the background.

Stage right will have two scenes. First will be the King Herod scene. To create this scene, place a large upholstered chair in the center of the area. Paint another insulation board gold and purple or cover it with gold and purple table cloths. This covering should look like drapery.

The scene with Mary and Joseph will be created by rotating the backdrop for King Herod. On the back of the Herod scenery, paint a Biblical era house. We have included a pattern and a design for this backdrop in the "3 Wise Men and a Baby Resource Kit."

The "2 Wise Men and a Baby" logo can hang behind the choir. You can download this logo art from the Lillenas website at www.lillenaskids.com. This back drop can be created by projecting the logo shape onto white paper. Trace the shape and paint. Cut the logo shape from insulation board and glue the logo created on the paper onto the piece of insulation. Attach the logo to a black stick, which has been placed in a flower pot filled with rocks. This will allow the logo to be free standing. This logo can also be projected with PowerPoint onto a screen behind the choir.

If you need a back drop for the entire stage behind the choir, create an outdoor Biblical scene. An example of this idea is available in the "3 Wise Men and a Baby" Resource Kit. After projecting the scene onto paper, trace and paint. Then glue the scene on to a piece of insulation board. The backdrops can be attached to dowel rods and placed in square flower pots filled with rocks.

To make the opening manger scene at center stage, have Joseph kneel next to a simple manger that he carries in.

To create the Jerusalem scene, make a sign on a post that says "Jerusalem." Create another sign that says "Bethlehem" on the opposite side of the Jerusalem sign. Place palm trees and ferns next to the sign. To create the Bethlehem scene, rotate the sign. You might want to add a simple well made by covering a large bucket in brown paper. Have Lydia and Martha move the well into place.

For more details about the set please consult the "3 Wise Men and a Baby Video" or the "3 Wise Men and a Baby Resource Kit."

Casting Ideas

Do you have a large, middle-sized, or small choir? Don't worry, this musical is perfect for any size choir. You may do the musical as written utilizing only the main characters if you have a smaller choir. If your choir is large, you may want to divide parts, or add solos. Be creative. Give everyone a part if possible. Giving every child some kind of special part will encourage attendance and participation.

Cast

"Three Wise Men and a Baby" can be cast in various ways. For a smaller choir, you may do the musical as written utilizing only the main characters. If your choir is large, you may want to divide parts, or add solos. Be creative. Give everyone a part if possible. Giving every child some kind of special part will encourage attendance and participation. Pray and God will lead you to the right decisions.

Wise Men 1 (Elvistonia)   _____

Wise Men 2 (Garthonia)   _____

Wise Men 3 (Jamestonia)   _____

Star   _____

Twink   _____

Sparklett   _____

Glow   _____

Scribe   _____

Lydia   _____

Martha   _____

Townsperson 1   _____

Townsperson 2   _____

Herod   _____

Mary *(Non-speaking role)*   _____

Joseph   _____

2 or 3 shepherds *(Non-speaking roles)*   _____

   _____

Townspeople *(optional)*   _____

   _____

Kid 1   _____

Kid 2   _____

Kid 3   _____

Kid 4   _____

Optional Cast

You may divide any part to create additional roles. You may add more stars and townspeople. Be creative. Do what works for your choir.

Specialty Dancers

To move or not to move? In an effort to supply the needs of all our churches, we are providing you with choreography for this children's choir musical. We realize that according to various denominations, this might or might not be appropriate for your church. We encourage you to seek the leadership of your church and seek the Lord in prayer as you make your decision. God bless YOU and know we are always here for questions or comments.

Note: The movement for the Specialty Dances is found in the "3 Wise Men and a Baby Resource Kit" or on the "3 Wise Men and a Baby Video."

"3 Wise Men and a Baby Dance Team"   _____

_____

_____

_____

_____

Costumes

Austin Wise Man 1 (Elvistonia)   Elvis style jumpsuit with a cape and crown, gold and purple

Jonathan & Zach Wise Man 2 (Garthonia)   Cowboy outfit with a cape, gold and blue, cowboy hat with a crown on the brim.

Clayton Wisemen 3 (Jamestonia)   James Brown style costume with a cape and crown in gold and red

Star   White, gold, and silver star costume with a star halo. (Star is the lead star, so his/her costume should be flashy.)

none needed

Twink   White, gold, and silver star costume with a star halo

Sparklett   White, gold, and silver star costume, chef's apron and hat

Glow   White, gold, and silver star costume with a star halo

Scribe - *Colin*   Typical scribe biblical costume

Lydia - *Nicki*   Biblical costume

Martha *Jayde*   Biblical costume

Randy Townsperson 1 and 2 *Jonathan Green*   Biblical costume

Herod *Mason*   Kingly biblical costume of purple, gold, and silver, crown

Mary *Brooke*   Biblical costume, primarily blue

Joseph *Zeph*   Biblical costume, primarily browns and tans

Matthew Shepherds *Connor*   Biblical costume, primarily browns and tans and stripes

Townspeople *(optional)*   Various biblical costumes

Kids 1-4   Star T-shirts and jeans

none needed

Choir   Star T-shirts and jeans.

The inexpensive star T-shirts can be purchased from Personalized Gifts and Apparel at 1-800-898-6170 or info@pg4u.com.

Specialty Dancers   See the "3 Wise Men and a Baby Resource Kit."

Set Design

The following is the layout of the set.

"3 Wise Men and a Baby" Backdrop

risers   risers

Star Backdrop   Bethlehem/Jerusalem   Herod/Joseph's Backdrop

soloists   soloists

X X   X X

Props

manger
shepherd's staffs
birthday cake with unlit candles
birthday cake with lit candles
sparkles
clipboard and pencil
wrapping paper, ribbon, and box
crown (optional)
sweater (optional)
tie (optional)
watch (optional)
3 stick camels
2 water pots
gold
box of frankincense
myrrh in a bag

Solos

Overture	No Solo
Jesus is Born	Solo
Go, Tell It On the Mountain	No Solo
We Three Kings	3 Solos (Wise Men)
Lookin' for a King	2 Solos
Star, Lead us to Jesus	Solo
Rockin' Baby Jesus	No Solo
I Can Only Imagine	Solo
The Best Gift is Me	Solo
Finale	No Solo
Curtain Call	No Solo

Microphones

It would be good to have a cordless lapel microphone for each main character. Hand-held microphones can be used as a substitute. Place three solo microphones on stands stage left.

Scripture References

Overture	*Luke 1:68*
Jesus is Born	*Luke 2:12*
Go, Tell It On the Mountain	*Luke 2:11, Luke 2:17*
We Three Kings	*Matthew 2:1*
Lookin' for a King	*Micah 5:2*
Star, Lead us to Jesus	*Matthew 2:2*
Rockin' Baby Jesus	*Luke 2:16-18*
I Can Only Imagine	*John 14:1-4*
The Best Gift is Me	*1 Corinthians 15:58, Mark 12:30 Romans 10:9-10*
Finale	*Matthew 2:11*
Curtain Call	*Matthew 5:16*

A Children's Christmas Musical teaching
that the best gift is me!

A Children's Christmas Musical teaching
that the best gift is me!

created by
Pam Andrews